MW01174177

Afternoon Tea

Drawings by

GLEN G. GREENWALT

Afternoon Tea

A Tea-Lover's Introduction

Every morning, I brew a dainty cup of tea to help me meditate, setting the mood for the day's dose of prose-making; every night, I sip another cup, calming my mind and body for peaceful slumber. Tea punctuates the rhythm of my daily life, enhancing its tone, brightening its mood.

I live this way merely based on our ancient belief that one must depend only on seven earthly elements for simple living and no more: wood, rice, oil, salt, soy-sauce, vinegar and tea. But to mind one's soul, six extra earthly things one must be endowed with: music, chess, prose, painting, poetry and wine.

This I abide by meekly and faithfully.

Little wonder I can't start a day's work without that steaming cup of soulfulness; and can't fall asleep without that cup of serenity.

Tea hence is my little deity and my little tyrant; my master and my servant all at the same time.

—Da Chen
Author of *My Last Empress*

Author's Note

The drawings in the three-book series — *Morning Coffee*, *Afternoon Tea*, and *Evening Wine* — grew out of my observations of people who come together to swap stories with friends, laugh, debate politics, interview for a job, read the paper or a book, or simply stare out of the window.

I have taught college religion and philosophy, but in my forties, at the encouragement of a colleague, I purchased a sketchbook. Drawing provided me a way of observing life with greater care than my own casual observations or academic studies had ever disclosed. At fifty-five, I finished a graduate degree in figurative studies.

I could draw a perfect likeness of a model holding a pose over several hours, but to learn how to draw people in motion, I began sketching in my local New York City coffee shop. Later, I moved out west, where I added several tea houses and a bistro to my favorite places to draw.

At first, I would hide the fact that I was drawing people. But they always noticed, and almost without exception, they were flattered, often adjusting their clothing or hair. If anyone appeared uncomfortable, or too posed, I would move on. I simply wanted to capture the everyday moments of life that usually go unobserved, to record how tea, coffee, and wine are the lubricants of social interaction, or of sweet solitude.

These books are a celebration of shared moments in our lives through my pen and ink — accompanied by the words of wiser people than I.

Glen Greenwalt, Seattle, 2012

Come, let us have some tea and continue
to talk about happy things.

CHAIM POTOK

There are few hours in life more
agreeable than the hour dedicated to
the ceremony of afternoon tea.

HENRY JAMES

glen greenwalt
2008

Is there no Latin word for Tea?
Upon my soul, if I had known that I
would have let the vulgar stuff alone.

Hilaire Belloc

There is no trouble so great or grave
that cannot be much diminished by
a nice cup of tea.

BERNARD-PAUL HEROUX

glen greenwalt
2011

Tea is a cup of life.

AUTHOR UNKNOWN

glen greenwalt
2009

Time for you and time for me,
And time yet for a hundred indecisions,
And for a hundred visions and revisions,
Before the taking of a toast and tea.

T. S. ELIOT

glen greenwalt
2011

It ought to be illegal for an artist to marry.
If the arist must marry let him find someone
more interested in art, or his art, or the artist
part of him, than him. After which let them
take tea together three times a week.

Ezra Pound

There is a great deal of poetry and
fine sentiment in a chest of tea.

RALPH WALDO EMERSON

glen greenwalt
2008

…Little Princess…It's always Tea-time…

Lewis Carroll

glen greenwalt
2009

I always fear that creation will
expire before teatime.

<small>SYDNEY SMITH</small>

Stands the church clock at ten to three?
And is there honey still for tea?

RUPERT BROOKE

glen greenwalt
2009

May you always have walls for the winds,
a roof for the rain, tea beside the fire, laughter
to cheer you, those you love near you, and
all your heart might desire.

IRISH BLESSING

glen greenwalt
2009

Find yourself a cup of tea.
The teapot is behind you.
Now tell me about hundreds
Of things.

Saki

glen greenwalt
2008

You can never get a cup of tea large enough
or a book long enough to suit me.

C. S. Lewis

glen greenwalt
200?

Tea should be taken in solitude.

Author Unknown

A NEW DAY

glen greenwalt
2009

Strange how a cup of tea can represent at the same time, the comforts of solitude, and the pleasures of company.

glen greenwalt
2009

My Dear, if you give me a cup of tea to clear my muddle of a head I should better understand your affairs.

CHARLES DICKENS

glen greenwalt
2011

Tea is liquid wisdom.

AUTHOR UNKNOWN

Picture you on my knee,
just tea two,
and two for tea.

IRVING CAESAR

Better to be deprived of food for three days,
than tea for one.

ANCIENT CHINESE PROVERB

glen greenwalt
2011

It is not that we should ignore the claims of posterity, but that we should seek to enjoy the present more.

KAKUZO OKAKURA

glen greenwalt
2009

Tea — the cups that cheer but not inebriate.

WILLIAM COWPER

glen greenwelt
2008

Great love affairs start with champagne
and end with tea.

HONORE' DE BALZAC

glen greenwalt
2010

Tea...is a religion of the art of life.

KAKUZO OKAKURA

glen greenwalt
2009

Ecstasy is a glass full of tea and a piece
of sugar in the mouth.

ALEXANDER PUSHKIN

glengreenwalt
2009

Tea is drunk to forget the din of the world.

T'ien Yiheng

glen greenwalt
2010

We had a kettle; we let it leak:
Our not repairing made it worse.
We haven't had any tea for a week...
The bottom is out of the Universe.

RUDYARD KIPLING

glen greenwalt
2008

"Take some more tea," the March Hare
said to Alice very earnestly.

"I've had nothing yet, "Alice replied in
an offended tone, "So I can't take more."

LEWIS CARROLL

glen greenwalt
2011

Where there is tea there's hope.

ARTHUR W. PINERO

glen greenwalt
2010

There is something in the nature
of tea that leads us into a world of
quiet contemplation of life.

Yutang Lin

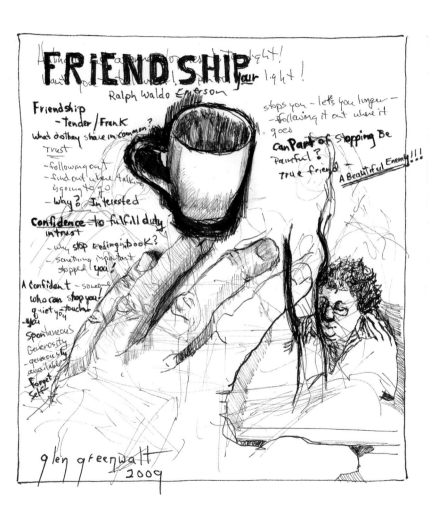

FRIENDSHIP _your light!_

Ralph Waldo Emerson

Friendship
- tender/frank
What do they share in common?
Trust
- following out
- find out where talking
  is going to go
- why? Interested

Confidence - to fulfill duty
intrust
- why stop reading in book?
- something important
  stopped you!

A Confidant - someone
who can stop you -
quiet you - touch
- you
Spontaneous
Generosity
- generously
  available
Forget
Self!

stops you - lets you linger -
- following it out where it
  goes
Can Part of Stopping Be
Painful?
true friend -
A Beautiful Enemy!!!

glen greenwalt
2009

I am in no way interested in immortality,
but only in the taste of tea.

Lu Tung Pin

Boservie from

glengreenwalt
2009

Tea, though ridiculed by those who are naturally course in their nervous sensibilities... will always be the favored beverage of the intellectual.

THOMAS DE QUINCEY

The scattered tea goes with the leaves
and every sunset dies.

BAUHAUS FOUNDER
WALTER GROPIUS

glen greenwalt
2011

If one has no tea, one is incapable
of understanding truth and beauty.

JAPANESE PROVERB

glen greenwalt
2010

The mere clink of cups and saucers
tunes the mind to happy repose.

George Gissing

greg greenwalt
2011

Bread and water can so easily be toast and tea.

AUTHOR UNKNOWN

glen greenwalt
2011

We will see if tea and buns can
make the world better.

KENNETH GRAHAME

glen greenwalt
2010

Love and scandal are the best sweeteners of tea.

HENRY FIELDING

glen greenwalt
2010

To a philosopher all news, as it is called,
is gossip, and they who edit and read
it are old women over their tea.

HENRY DAVID THOREAU

glengreenwalt
2010

All true tea lovers not only like their tea strong, but like it a little stronger with each year that passes.

George Orwell

Black Iced Tea
and Ginger Lemonade
che - vegetarian
ata - Sausage, Leeks, fe
Spinach, fontin
Soups
Tomato Bisque

glen greenwalt
2010

If you are cold, tea will warm you.
If you are heated, it will cool you.
If you are depressed, it will cheer you.
If you are excited, it will calm you.

WILLIAM EWART GLADSTONE

glen greenwalt
·2010

Each cup of tea represents an imaginary voyage.

HENRY JAMES

ESPRESSO ★ TEA ★ PASTRI

glen greenwalt
2010

Acknowledgements

I would like to thank my teachers at the New York Academy of Art who taught me the rules of proportions and the construction of a beautiful form. Martha Mason, who through her own drawings taught me the beauty and energy of scribbling. Karen Fields, who watching me draw in a coffee shop, first suggested that my sketches should be published alongside quotations about coffee.

Helen Zimmermann, my agent, who believed in my project and transformed the idea I had for a regional book on Saturday mornings in my local coffee shop into three books, Morning Coffee, Afternoon Tea, and Evening Wine. Without her perseverance, as well as that of Carl Lennertz, this project would never have found a home with the wonderful people at Delphinium Books who made this dream come true. Thank you to Kathleen Servidio at HarperCollins for a beautiful book design.

Finally, I would like to thank the people who encouraged me throughout this project: my parents, Don and Rose Greenwalt; my sister Linda Tonsberg; my children, Natascha and Gavin, who are each successful artists in their own right; Dan Lamberton and Ron Jolliffe, who listened to hours of my worries; and Elena Mezisko, who not only encouraged me in this project, but added sparkle to my life.

About the Author

GLEN G. GREENWALT holds a PhD from Vanderbilt University and graduated Cum Laude from the New York Academy of Art. He has been teaching for over 20 years, currently as Adjunct Professor of Humanities at Shasta College in California.

The drawings in the three books grew out of studied observations of people who come together for social contact at coffee houses, tea rooms, and bistros. His quest was to explore and share this core experience of life through his drawings and the quotes he selected.